MW00930740

To Randi –
wishing you the
very best!
Blessings and love,

Steven Moore

THEODORE THUMBS

Written by Steven T. Moore - Illustrated by Morgan Davis

Published by
Clear Fork Publishing
P.O. Box 870
102 S. Swenson
Stamford, Texas 79553
Phone: (325)773-5550
Fax: (325)773-5551
clearforkpublishing.com

Printed and Bound in the United States of America.

ISBN - 978-0-9895568-5-7
Library of Congress - 2016934306

For my parents,
Troy and Clara L. Moore
— Steven

For my nephews and niece
Jackson, Ben, and Ruby
— Morgan

Once upon a time in a town
not too far away from yours

there lived a young boy named Theodore Thumbs.

He would always walk around town
on the happy, sunny sidewalks...

...where people small and tall
would look down on this
little boy with his
thumb in his mouth.

He drew attention from those near and far because he was small and skinny, his clothes would drag along whenever he walked, and because his long hair had a life of its own.

He was old enough to talk, but when they would

laugh, point, and stare,

he would always, as his body shook in fear,

believe in his lucky thumb.

One day while walking upon the sunlit sidewalks, he left his thumb by his side on the way to school, just down the street,

past the grocery store on his left,

past the crooked little church in the distance,

...past his favorite Hamburger and Ice-cream Shoppe.

"Hello, Theodore Thumbs!"
His teacher said with a cheer of
sunshine in her voice.

She always smiled and greeted her
students as they hiked through the door.

"How are you?"
"I'm okay," Theodore said
with a half little smile.

But on the way to his desk,

he tripped over his clothes.

Books, pencils, and papers went everywhere.

Everyone laughed, pointed, and stared.

Theodore quietly sat down at his desk.

He nervously looked around. Then he nervously looked down.

He placed his thumb in his mouth and listened for the lesson of the day.

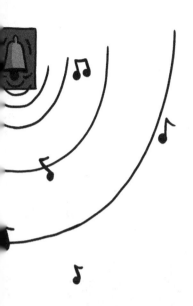

After the lesson, the kids
all of a sudden heard
a happy sound.

The recess bell rang throughout the playground as kids roamed around like creatures from the city zoo.

The brown oak trees were warmly embraced with little hands and little feet.

Some boys flew from one long branch to the next and some girls skipped around in fields of tall green grass and white sticky flowers.

Instead of joining
the boys by the
trees, Theodore ran
over to the slide and
swing set, and then
he sadly sat there
on the swing by
himself.

While sitting there, a crowd of kids surrounded him.

The kids began yelling cruel things at him.

"Why do you wear
those ugly clothes all
the time?"

"You look so silly
sitting there!"

"Why is your hair so
weird and funny?"

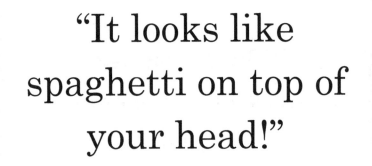

"It looks like spaghetti on top of your head!"

Theodore jumped off
the swing and just
stood there.
Stood there without
saying a word.

They all laughed.
They all pointed.
They all stared.

Then they began chanting and singing,
"Look at silly Theodore Thumbs!
Look at silly Theodore Thumbs!"

Over and over again, they
kept singing this sad song
about his name.

He nervously looked around...

He nervously looked down...

His body shook in fear...

Then he placed his thumb in his mouth.

When school was over, Theo ran as fast as he could.

His tears began falling down on the sad, sunny sidewalks...

He ran and he ran...past his favorite
Hamburger and Ice-cream Shoppe,
past the crooked little church,

past the grocery store...

He sat down by his favorite tree in the front yard of his house.

Theo's parents finally came out to see him, and they
quickly asked about his day.

After he shared with them about his horrible day, they responded.
"Ignore them! Ignore them, no matter what they say!"
"If they laugh, point, and stare, remember that
you are very, very special."

"No!" they shouted.
"You are more than special...
You are thumbtastic!"

"Thumbtastic?" Theo wondered.

"Yes, you are thumbtastic, more than fantastic!"

With that said, Theodore Thumbs smiled
the biggest smile.
"I'm thumbtastic! I'm thumbtastic!"
He said over and over again.

Then everyone in the neighborhood joined in with his parents.

They all cheered.
They all smiled.
They all applauded.

For dear little Theodore Thumbs...

Then they began chanting and singing,

"Look at Thumbtastic!"

"Look at Thumbtastic!"

Over and over again, they kept singing this happy

song about his name.

So remember, my dear friend, when they start making fun of you, when you are having a bad day, remember that you are...

CPSIA information can be obtained
at www.ICGtesting.com
Printed in the USA
LVHW061555230620
658804LV00003B/18